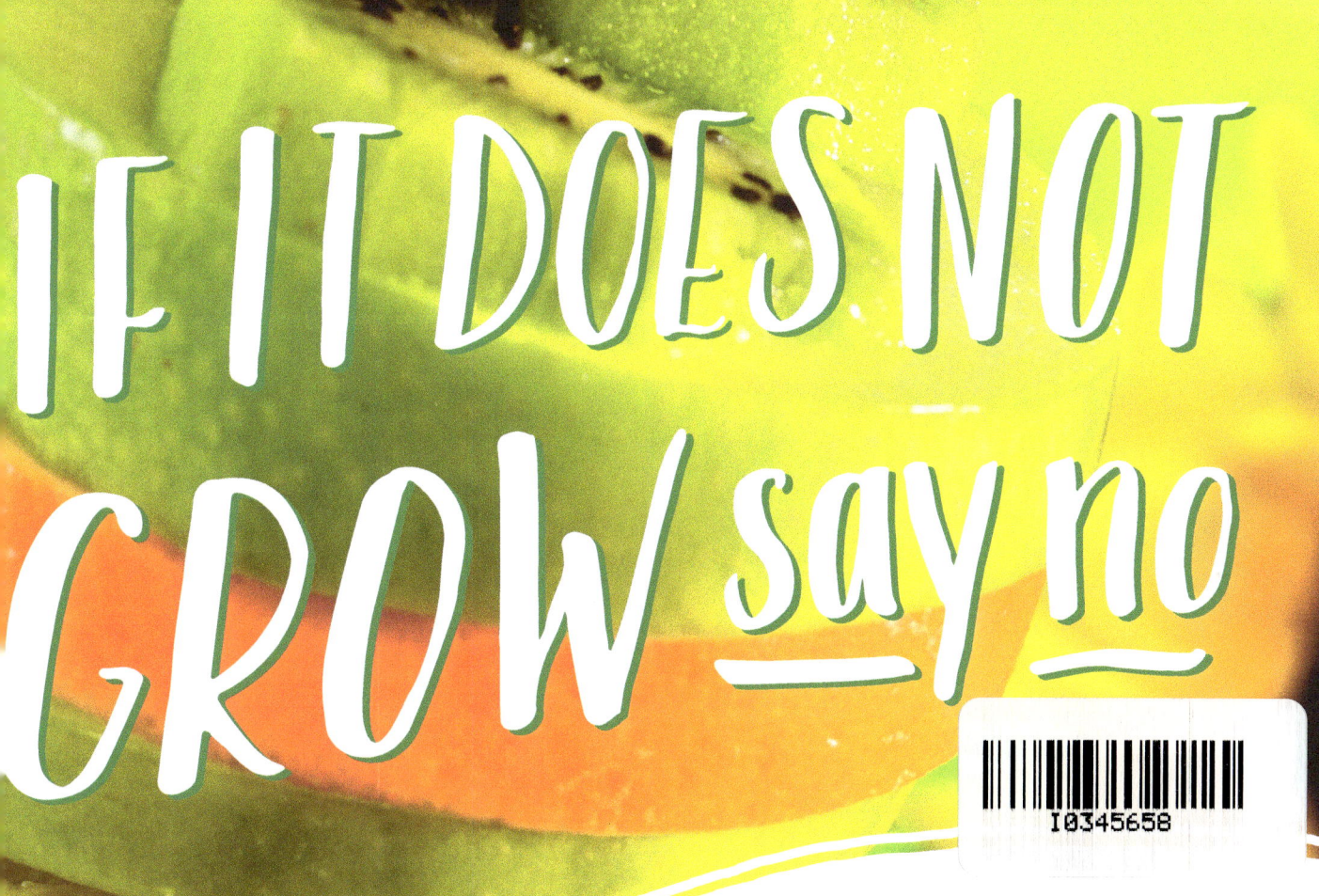

IF IT DOES NOT GROW say no

Eatable Activities for Kids

by KERRY ALISON WEKELO

Copyright © 2015 by Kerry Alison Wekelo
All rights reserved.
No part of this book may be reproduced, copied, stored or transmitted in any form or by any means - graphic, electronic or mechanical, including photocopying, without the prior written permission of Peaceful Daily, Inc. and
Kerry Alison Wekelo except where permitted by law.
Published by Peaceful Daily, Inc.
www.peacefuldaily.com

ISBN 978-0-9970143-6-5

EISBN 978-0-9970143-7-2

Printed in the United States of America.
First Edition
10 9 8 7 6 5 4 3 2 1

DEDICATION

To my amazing kids, Audrey and Blaine, who inspire me daily. They worked closely with me on the book: Audrey provided editing and layout ideas, and Blaine created the dessert challenge. This book has been a tool for us to do our best at being healthy together. We are not perfect, yet we strive.

To my Dad, for taking the amazing pictures in the book to make the food come alive. You have consistently led by example, and, as I tell everyone, you are the healthiest person I know.

CREDITS

Creative Design: *Jacqueline Smith*
Editing: *Starla King*
Photography: *Al Wekelo*

INTRODUCTION

Kids and healthy foods tend to mix like oil and water, but what happens when you add fun and adventure? Suddenly kids are interested in their fruits and vegetables, curious about their health and eating, and even willing to try some healthy foods they usually consider "ewwwww!" In our society today, we tend to make food the enemy. *If It Does Not Grow – Say No* is one way for kids to make food – healthy food – a friend again. Activities include drawing, writing, cooking, and other puzzles that help kids learn about and enjoy healthy eating.

Healthy eating is not just about what we eat, but how and why we eat it. Use this activity book to help teach kids (and grown-ups!) to slow down for mealtimes, to pay more attention to fruits and veggies, and to make conscious choices for their health. These are lessons that naturally spread into other areas of their lives, making them stronger, healthier, happier kids.

What we eat provides energy to make our bodies strong and healthy. What activities do you love? Draw or write about them here.

Eating a balanced rainbow of food helps us make sure we are getting all our vitamins and minerals*. Circle the foods you enjoy.

*Vitamins and minerals are stored in our food. We need them to grow and develop properly, and each vitamin has a special role in our health. Some examples are:

- Vitamin A in carrots helps with our sight.
- Vitamin C in oranges helps our body heal when we get cut.
- B vitamins in whole grains help our body make energy from food.

TIP:
Make a rainbow fruit kabob (fruit on a stick) with raspberries, oranges, pineapples, kiwi, blueberries, and grapes.

Fruits and vegetables have beautiful colors. Name as many fruits and vegetables you can think of in each color below.

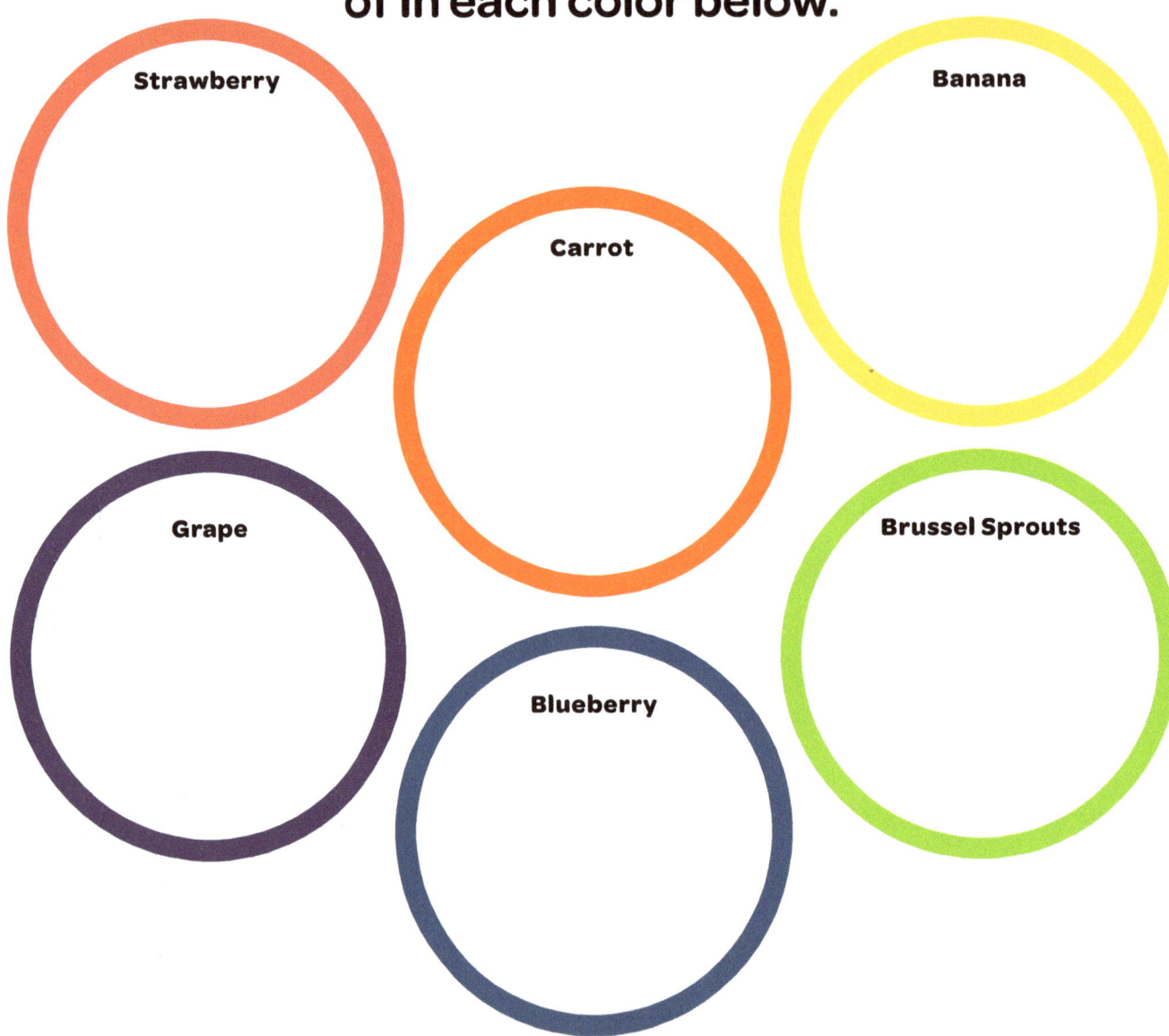

TIP:

Eat fruits and vegetables during their growing seasons.
Winter: *Oranges, grapefruit, sweet potatoes, squash*
Spring: *Bananas, strawberries, spinach, green beans*
Summer: *Berries, cantaloupe, corn, peppers, cucumbers*
Fall: *Pears, cranberries, broccoli, carrots, pumpkin*

Eating a variety of colorful foods is an easy way to make sure you have a well-balanced diet to keep your bodies and brains happy. Can you create a meal using all colors of the rainbow? Write the menu below (include the food colors!)

Who would you invite to your rainbow meal?

Apples are one of the healthiest fruits because they have a lot of fiber, which helps with digestion. That's why people say, "An apple a day keeps the doctor away." What is your favorite way to eat apples?

RAW APPLES

Make an apple sandwich with your favorite toppings. Spread peanut, almond or sunflower butter on an apple slice to make it sticky. Add any toppings you like, such as pumpkin seeds, almonds, raisins, dried cranberries or blueberries, granola or honey. Put another apple slice on top. See if you can eat it without the insides squishing out!

BAKED APPLES

Cut up an apple, then place in a baking dish. Sprinkle with cinnamon. Add 2-4 tablespoons of water (2 for small apple, 3 for medium, 4 for large). Get creative and add other goodies such as your favorite nuts or dried fruit. Bake for 10-15 minutes at 350 degrees.

Broccoli is one of the world's healthiest foods because it makes your bones and heart strong, and helps your body fight off sickness. Color your favorite part of broccoli.

TIP:
High-fiber foods, such as fruits and vegetables, help your digestive system break food up and move it around (and out of!) your body easily.

BROCCOLI RECIPE

Take a bunch of broccoli and cut it into any size you want. For the best tasting broccoli, steam it by cooking in hot water for 5 minutes. Test these seasonings: Garlic salt, lemon pepper or lemon juice.

What are your favorite vegetables? Create a vegetable kabob, and write down the vegetables in the order you stacked them on the stick.

TIP: Vegetables are easier to digest if they are cooked.

BAKING KABOBS:
Place kabobs on a baking sheet and drizzle with an oil and seasoning of your choice. Oils: Almond, Coconut or Olive. Seasoning: Garlic salt blend, black pepper, lemon pepper or lemon and lime juice. Bake until they're as soft as you like them, about 10-15 minutes at 400 degrees.

If you could use a piece of fruit as a boat, which would you choose? Write about or draw it below.

TIP 2:

Did you know that 75% of what you weigh is actually from water? It's important to give your body enough fluids every day so it keeps working smoothly.

TIP 1:

Very juicy fruits that get most of their weight from the juice have a high "water weight." Did the fruit you chose have a high water weight? Watermelon and strawberries have the highest, around 92%, and other fruits such as bananas, peaches, pineapples, grapes, oranges, and pears have 75%-88% water weight.

What do you know about eating fruits and vegetables? Check off the correct answers.

	Yes	No
Each meal should be half fruits and vegetables.		
I should eat my food quickly.		
Fruits and vegetables contain vitamins and minerals.		
It is okay to use a vitamin instead of eating fruits and vegetables.		
Fruits and vegetables are high in water weight.		
Broccoli is one of the healthiest foods.		
Vitamins and minerals help our bodies stay healthy and fight off sickness.		
Fruits and vegetables help our body to naturally repair when we do get sick.		
It is okay if I don't eat enough fruits and vegetables.		
The skin on fruits and vegetables has NO nutritional value.		
I should eat my food slowly and mindfully.*		

* MINDFUL EATING:

As you eat your food, try to think of all the people who made it possible. For example, the person who planted the seed, the person who bagged the groceries, and your parent for buying the food. To fully experience all the different flavors of food, eat slowly, and pause after each bite.

Are you brave?

 **YES**

Which fruit will you try that you have never tried?

Which vegetable?

What did the new fruit or vegetable taste like?

NO

Why not?

TIP:
One medium-sized sweet potato has about 438% of the vitamin A and 37% of the vitamin C you need each day. It also contains calcium, potassium, and iron.

BAKING SWEET POTATOES:
The best way to bake a sweet potato is to place it in about 1 inch of water in a baking dish. Make one slit down the sweet potato, cover with aluminum foil, and bake for 45 minutes to 1 hour at 350 degrees. Try these seasonings: cinnamon, cardamom, or nutmeg.

Food is fun! You can dice it or slice it, and some of it even rolls all over. Draw a picture made out of fruit and vegetable shapes. If you have permission, try making a picture using real fruits and vegetables!

TIP:

Imagine a banana as an airplane or tree trunk, use blueberries as eyes, cucumbers to make a snake, or bananas and raisins to make a smiley face.

We need protein because it builds, takes care of, and replaces the tissues in our body. Our muscles, organs, and immune system are made up of mostly protein.

Find and circle the sources of protein in the word search below.

- Legumes
- Black Beans
- Lentils
- Nuts
- Almonds
- Cashews
- Seeds
- Pumpkin
- Sunflower
- Broccoli
- Spinach
- Oatmeal
- Cauliflower
- Nut butters

C	A	U	L	I	F	L	O	W	E	R	O	W
B	D	L	X	Z	V	W	W	S	Q	A	S	J
U	L	V	S	E	E	D	S	U	U	L	U	C
X	P	A	W	C	J	O	P	N	H	M	Q	V
J	B	P	C	A	H	I	Q	F	I	O	B	B
H	L	P	Y	K	R	T	L	L	L	N	R	K
Y	B	U	G	O	A	G	V	O	E	D	O	O
K	C	M	N	G	E	L	A	W	N	S	C	D
S	U	P	O	X	C	H	U	E	T	N	C	F
P	H	K	B	D	O	A	R	R	I	U	O	U
I	W	I	V	C	W	U	S	K	L	T	L	B
N	L	N	O	K	N	C	K	H	S	S	I	E
A	Z	E	F	A	B	U	T	T	E	R	S	A
C	E	T	G	V	T	J	T	J	P	W	A	N
H	J	L	P	U	E	M	O	S	Z	T	S	S
N	U	C	D	R	M	G	E	R	P	O	F	Y
F	D	W	F	Z	U	E	L	A	A	P	E	X
B	U	L	E	B	F	L	S	Q	L	C	N	E
P	Y	N	N	J	H	M	L	W	Q	M	Y	F

RECIPE:

Make a trail mix with your favorite nuts and dried fruit for a high protein snack.

Whole grains are necessary for creating energy in our bodies. Did you know that whole grains contain every part of the grain?

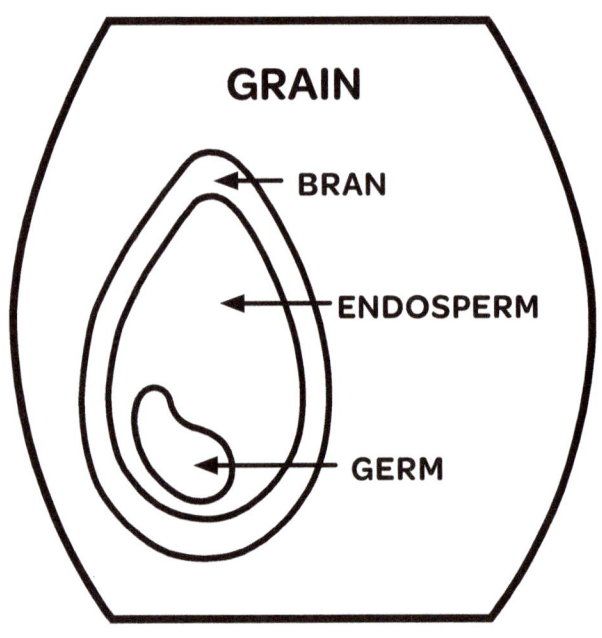

Processed, white grains are not whole grains because they are missing a part. The bran, where many of the nutrients are stored, is removed, so **white grains are less healthy.**

RECIPES:
- **Use whole wheat tortillas to make wraps such as fruit and nut butter or vegetable combinations.**
- **Add fruit or nuts to oatmeal.**

List examples of the different types of grains. Circle your favorites.

Whole Grains	White Grains
Example: Whole Wheat Bread	**White Bread**

How much sugar did you eat today? How much was "natural" sugar from fruits, and how much was "processed" sugar from candies or cookies? List your sugar foods below, then look at the labels on each food to list how many grams of sugar per serving.*

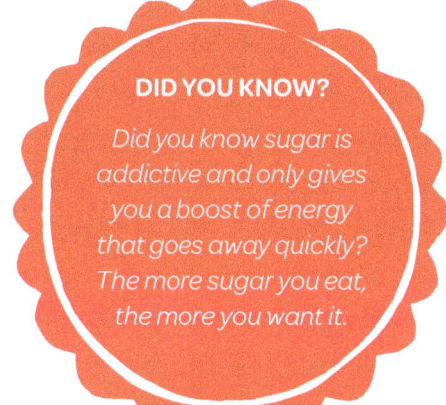

DID YOU KNOW?

Did you know sugar is addictive and only gives you a boost of energy that goes away quickly? The more sugar you eat, the more you want it.

NATURAL ☺	PROCESSED ☹
Breakfast (Cantaloupe)	Cereal
Lunch (Carrots)	Cookie
Dinner (Corn)	Ice Cream
Snacks (Apple)	Gummy Fruit Snacks

NOTE: The American Heart Association recommends no more than 3 teaspoons (12 grams) per day for kids, 5 teaspoons (20 grams) for adult women, and 9 teaspoons (36 grams) for adult men.

Describe a time when you ate too much sugar. How did you feel?

DID YOU KNOW?

Our bodies use sugar to get quick energy, but the energy doesn't last long because sugar tells our body to release insulin, a chemical that quickly brings down the level of sugar in our blood. Too much sugar can make our moods and energy levels go up and down like a rollercoaster. It can even give us a headache or make us feel sick.

Why do you want to be strong and healthy? Draw or write about it.

Where does food come from? Can you name all the places and people that help get food to you?

What have you learned from this book?

What change will you make so you eat healthy foods and do healthy activities?

Fruit Tasting Challenge: Track new fruits you try.

Type of Fruit	What did it taste like?	What did it feel like when you touched it? Tasted it?	Did you like it? (Yes or No)

Vegetable Tasting Challenge: Track new veggies you try.

Type of Veggie	What did it taste like?	What did it feel like when you touched it? Tasted it?	Did you like it? (Yes or No)

Dessert Challenge:
Try different fruit combinations as dessert for one week. Get your whole family to help come up with healthy combinations.

MONDAY	
TUESDAY	
WEDNESDAY	
THURSDAY	
FRIDAY	
SATURDAY	
SUNDAY	

IDEAS:
- Mix fresh and dried fruits
- Use honey for a little extra sweetness
- Try spices such as cinnamon, ginger, and nutmeg

www.ingramcontent.com/pod-product-compliance
Lightning Source LLC
Chambersburg PA
CBHW061937290426
44113CB00025B/2941